Step into the Arena

Show Up and Lead

Chuck Anderson, Major General
(Retired) U.S. Army

Military Might Publishing

Copyright @ 2025 by Chuck Anderson

All rights reserved.

No portion of this book may be reproduced in any form without written permission from the publisher or author, except as permitted by U.S. copyright law.

Publisher's Cataloging-in-Publication Data

Names: Anderson, Charles Allan ("Chuck"), 1958- .
Title: Step into the arena : show up and lead / Chuck Anderson.
Description: Colorado Springs, CO : Military Might Publishing, 2025. | Summary: A no-excuses, action-driven guide to leadership and life that encourages the reader to step into the arena, own your moment, and lead with discipline, grit, and presence, every single day.
Identifiers: ISBN 9781961019256
Subjects: LCSH: Leadership. | Discipline. | Reliability. | Perseverance (Ethics). | BISAC: SELF-HELP / Self-Management / General. | SELF-HELP / Personal Growth / General. | SELF-HELP / Motivational & Inspirational.
Classification: LCC HM1261 . A53 2025 | DDC 303.34--dc23

DEDICATION

I dedicate this book to Coach Herb Conley, Ashland Tomcats, U.S Army Colonel (Retired) Vincent Tedesco, and U.S Army Sergeant Major (R) Rufus Allen. All are positive inflection points on this obstacle course we call Life. Above all, this book and this life is not possible without my teammate and wife Tammy. Tammy is always by my side and shows up daily in the Arena. She is a true Spartan who places family (Robert and Sara) first and creates memories for generations to come in the Anderson family. I am the best version of myself because of my faith, family, and friends. All made possible, by showing up.

FORWARD

While I had met Chuck Anderson previously my first opportunity to work closely with him was in the spring of 1994 and thus began the start of a long professional relationship and close friendship. We would continue to serve and work together in various parts of the world to include Chuck serving as my chief of staff during a combat deployment in the Mideast. We have continued our relationship in our post military careers through today.

In a rapidly changing world where many are looking for an understanding of how to self-improve, find success for themselves or how to make positive changes for their organization or in their own lives, Chuck provides answers. He lays out simple yet fresh ideas and common-sense approaches that guarantee success whatever your goals.

Chuck brings a unique set of skills, based in advanced education, leadership experiences and equally if not more important real-life experiences that make him extremely well qualified to share his ideas with others. He does not derive these methods solely from classroom instruction, Chuck has lived these methods and I have witnessed his success as a result. From teaching physical fitness classes at West Point, to leading Soldiers of all ages and ranks, to turning around companies, he has used and developed the techniques described in the book with the upmost success.

For over 30 years I have personally watched Chuck live the methods he is now sharing and witness the positive impact on others. As we prepared our organization for a combat deployment he used these methods to train, develop and build a newly organized staff to the highest level of proficiency and a coherent focused team. Many of the individuals confided in me how Chuck had personally helped them achieve new heights both personally and professionally that they never thought possible. He has done this in every organization, miliary or civilian wherever he has been. I have personally benefited more than once from his approach to overcoming complex challenges.

One of the more personal examples is his earlier work and compassion with special needs children as they prepared for the Special Olympics. His simple presence and energy demonstrates the breadth of his passion for being present and engaging when the most important to make a difference for others and yourself. To me this is just one example of how his model works for all.

> SO WHY READ THIS BOOK—AS THE WORLD CONTINUES TO MOVE FASTER AND FASTER, A CONTINUED GROWTH OF TECHNOLOGY THAT BOTH ENHANCES AND SEPARATES OUR LIVES, PEOPLE CONTINUE TO STRIVE FOR PERSONAL AND PROFESSIONAL IMPROVEMENTS. THIS BOOK PROVIDES THAT ROAD MAP FOR SUCCESS THROUGH REAL LIFE. EXPERIENCES AND EXAMPLES. IT IS A REFRESHING SET OF INSIGHTS ALL FOUND ON A TRACK RECORD OF DEMONSTRATED POSITIVE RESULTS.

Chuck's methods provide a tested and proven path for success. By "Showing Up" a true impactful difference can be realized. On numerous occasions I have witnessed the author showing up and making a positive impact for people and organizations. So if you are looking for a meaningful and relevant guide to help build stronger relationships, improve your teams performance or help achieve your personal goals this book is where you must start.

───────────────────────────────────────

Howard Bromberg - served in the U.S Army for 37 years in a variety of leadership positions and served as the Director of Army Personnel before transitioning to civilian industry. He is a retired Lieutenant General and is now serving in the Defense Industry.

INTRODUCTION

Have you ever wondered how to rise above the noise, connect meaningfully in a disconnected world, or leave a lasting impact in both your personal and professional life? If so, this book is for you. It's not about abstract theories or overly complicated strategies—it's a roadmap for action. Whether you're starting your career, leading a team, or simply striving to be the best version of yourself, the principles in these pages will resonate deeply.

Success—true success—is rarely the result of one single factor. It's an intricate recipe of relationships, education, experience, and exposure. Add in hard work, perseverance, resiliency, and even a little luck, and you'll discover a path that's both unique and universal. But one critical attribute ties it all together: the ability to show up.

Over the course of 32 years in the United States Army and 14 years in the Federal Services Industry, I've learned that showing up—fully, intentionally, and prepared—has the power to transform not only your own life but also the lives of those around you. I've seen the difference it makes on the battlefield, in the boardroom, and around the dinner table. Showing up is your best foot forward, the first step in overcoming obstacles, seizing opportunities, and creating meaningful change.

What Does It Mean to Show Up?

Showing up is more than just being present. It's about bringing your full self—mentally, physically, and emotionally—into the arena. It's about being prepared, engaged, and ready to make a difference. In today's world, where virtual meetings and digital interactions have become the norm, it's easy to forget the irreplaceable value of human presence. Bottom Line Up Front—there is no substitute for Showing Up. Inflection points—the moments that change the trajectory of your life—don't happen in the cheap seats. They happen in the arena, where you face challenges head-on, learn from failure, and build resilience. Whether you're in the military, business, education, or simply navigating the complexities of family life, showing up isn't just respected—it's remembered.

Why This Book?

This isn't just a leadership guide or a manual for personal growth. It's both. It's for anyone striving to lead with purpose, build meaningful relationships, and navigate life's challenges with confidence. It's for anyone ready to unlock the power of showing up and harness it to create a better future.

> THROUGH REAL-LIFE STORIES, ACTIONABLE ADVICE, AND TIMELESS LESSONS, THIS BOOK WILL GIVE YOU THE TOOLS TO:
>
> - DEVELOP A PERSONAL CULTURE THAT DRIVES YOUR SUCCESS.
> - BUILD AND SUSTAIN MEANINGFUL RELATIONSHIPS.
> - MASTER RESILIENCE AND PERSEVERANCE TO OVERCOME SETBACKS AND CHALLENGES.
> - LEAD WITH INTEGRITY, HUMILITY, AND COURAGE.
> - THRIVE IN A WORLD OF REMOTE WORK AND DIGITAL CONNECTION.

As you read, you'll learn how to Prepare on Paper, identify your "Spartans," and recognize what right looks like. You'll discover how to push success down to your team, squint with your ears to listen deeply, and step into the arena with confidence. This is a guide for building a life of impact—one where showing up becomes your greatest advantage.

A Personal Journey

I grew up in Ashland, Kentucky, a town rooted in strong family values and community support. From there, my journey took me to the United States Military Academy at West Point, where I continued to develop perseverance and resilience that would shape my career. Over three decades in the Army, I moved 20 times with my family, led teams across continents, and learned invaluable lessons about leadership, teamwork, and perseverance. Transitioning to the Federal Services Industry, I oversaw more than 20,000 employees across 72 countries, managing $2.2 billion in annual revenue.

Through it all, one truth became clear: success begins with Showing Up.

The Time to Show Up Is Now

In 2020, the COVID-19 pandemic reshaped how we live and work. Remote connections became the norm, and while they offered convenience, they also revealed a stark truth: software cannot replace human presence. The power of Showing Up—physically, mentally, and emotionally—has never been more evident. It's what drives relationships, builds trust, and creates the conditions for success and happiness.

When the smoke clears from life's obstacle course, one thing remains: Showing Up is Rule #1. Mastering the fundamentals, preparing intentionally, and surrounding yourself with the right people—your Spartans—will set you on a path to lasting impact. This book is your guide to embracing that journey.

If you're ready to lead with purpose, strengthen your personal culture, and make an enduring impact, let's begin. Together, we'll explore what it truly means to show up—and why it's the key to living a life of meaning, fulfillment, and success.

TABLE OF CONTENTS

A CALL TO SHOW UP

1. Inflection Points—A Coach, a Battalion Commander, and a Platoon Sergeant 2
2. No Excuses, Show Up 10
3. Show Up in a Hybrid Environment 16

IN THE FIGHT

4. The Arena 24
5. Perseverance and Resiliency - Your Body Armor 32
6. Show Up Together—Teamwork 35

GEAR UP AND GO

7. Spartans—A Must-Have in the Arena 40
8. No Moonwalking—Problem Solving 46
9. Mastering the Basics - A Product of Showing Up 49

TABLE OF CONTENTS

IN THE ARENA

10.	Family and Friends	56
11.	Plate Spinners vs. Ball Jugglers	60
12.	Show-Up and Stay	65

LEAD THE WAY

13.	Show-Up and Be Happy	70
14.	Show-Up Roadmap	74
15.	Final Thoughts	81

ADDED CONTENT

About the author	83

A CALL TO

SHOW UP

01 INFLECTION POINTS—A COACH, A BATTALION COMMANDER, AND A PLATOON SERGEANT

As you journey through life, you encounter events that demand your action, decisions that shape your path ahead, and obstacles that challenge your resolve. We're all on a unique path, and along the way, there are pivotal moments that change our trajectory—what I call "inflection points." These moments can arise from people, experiences, or choices that leave a lasting impact. At times they can be unpredictable and can be positive or negative, but they always have the power to alter your course.

For me, three significant inflection points emerged early on: a high school football coach, a platoon sergeant, and my first battalion commander. These individuals left an indelible mark on my life, shaping my personal culture and influencing how I approached every challenge that lay ahead.

The Coach

In the summer of 1975, in Ashland, Kentucky, I was the quarterback for my high school football team.

This wasn't just any team—it was the Ashland Tomcats, and we were more than a group of athletes; we were a community, a brotherhood. Many of us had been playing together for years, growing up side by side in a town where everyone knew your name and your story. Ashland wasn't just a place on the map; it was a wholistic experience. Being a Tomcat football player was the pinnacle of our youth, and every bit of sweat, effort, and dedication was poured into achieving that dream.

Every summer, we prepared for the season with a week-long football camp in Tennessee. But long before that, we trained tirelessly in a no-frills, concrete-floored weight room beneath Putnam Stadium. There were no fancy machines—just free weights, raw determination, and an unyielding belief in the Tomcat tradition. The workouts were voluntary, but if you wanted to be ready for camp, you showed up.

At the heart of this effort was Coach Herb Conley. A legend in our town and beyond, Coach Conley was the embodiment of discipline. He was a role model, a leader, someone whose words matched his actions. His mantra was simple but profound: show up. Not just physically, but mentally and emotionally, ready to give your all.

One of his most memorable lessons came on a humid summer day. As we stood in that dimly lit weight room, he reminded us that success wasn't just about being present; it was about being fully engaged, ready to give everything you had. It was about preparing yourself so thoroughly that you were ready for whatever challenges came your way. And that lesson wasn't just about football—it was about life.

On game days, Coach Conley would gather us together, his voice filled with conviction, delivering pep talks that still resonate with me today. One such talk, directed at the kick-off team, was a turning point. He told us to run straight, not to veer around blockers but to push through them. If you got knocked down, you get back up and kept moving forward.

> THAT SIMPLE MESSAGE—TO FACE OBSTACLES HEAD-ON AND TO RISE AFTER EVERY FALL—BECAME A CORE PRINCIPLE IN MY LIFE. IN ESSENCE, EVERYDAY YOU ARE ON THE KICK-OFF TEAM!

The Battalion Commander

Fast forward six years to my first assignment as a young officer in the U.S. Army. Fresh out of West Point, I was eager to prove myself, ready to embrace the challenges ahead. I found myself in the 1/3 Air Defense Artillery Battalion, 101st Airborne Division at Fort Campbell, Kentucky. It was here that I encountered my next inflection point: my Battalion Commander.

On my first day of my first assignment in the United States Army, I was privileged to have an office call Colonel Vincent Tedesco, the Battalion Commander, and it was immediately clear that I was joining an exceptional unit led by an outstanding warfighter. Colonel Tedesco exuded a commanding presence and a genuine dedication to his soldiers. He was a leader who inspired and set high standards, someone who truly cared about his troops and their assigned mission.

The Battalion Commander's influence was profound. He embodied what it meant to be a dedicated, inspirational leader who set the example in every way. His leadership style reinforced the idea that success wasn't just about being in charge but about caring and setting the example for your soldiers, knowing your mission, and being tactically and technically competent. Under his command, I learned the importance of leading with purpose and conviction, traits that would serve me throughout my military and civilian career.

The Platoon Sergeant

It was in that same unit that I met my second inflection point: SFC Rufus Allen, Platoon Sergeant. SFC Allen was a Vietnam veteran—tall, technically and tactically competent, and a phenomenal leader. On my first day, he laid out everything I needed to know about the platoon, from personnel to equipment, training schedules to strengths and weaknesses. He told me that if I listened to him, I'd become the best platoon leader in the battalion. And he wasn't wrong.

His guidance echoed my football coach's teachings: show up. Be there for every physical training session, every maintenance day, and every training event.

> BUT IT WASN'T JUST ABOUT BEING PRESENT;
> IT WAS ABOUT BEING FULLY ENGAGED,
> LEARNING EVERY ASPECT OF THE
> PLATOON FROM THE GROUND UP.

SFC Allen insisted that I become proficient with every weapon we had in the platoon, even those I wasn't assigned to use. His reasoning was simple: in combat, you needed to be prepared for the unexpected.

This hands-on approach extended to equipment maintenance. Almost every Saturday morning, my Platoon Sergeant would have me join him in the motor pool, teaching me how to perform preventive maintenance checks and services. He wasn't training me to be a mechanic; he was preparing me to be a competent leader who understood operator knowledge of every piece of equipment in the platoon.

The impact of SFC Allen's mentorship was immediate and profound. Under his guidance, I became not just a platoon leader, but a leader who showed up—prepared, knowledgeable, and ready to contribute to the mission. His insistence on mastering the fundamentals made me one of the best platoon leaders in the battalion, just as he'd promised.

The Power of Showing Up

Reflecting on these three inflection points, it's clear they were more than just a coach, a commander, and a platoon sergeant—they were architects of my personal culture. They taught me that showing up wasn't just about being physically present; it was about being fully committed, prepared, and ready to face any challenge head-on.

Inflection points are rarely obvious in the moment. They might seem like just another practice, another training session, another piece of advice. But over time, they shape who you are, how you think, and how you approach life. These moments, these people, become the foundation of your personal culture, guiding you as you navigate the twists and turns of your journey.

As I continued my career, both in the Army and later in the business world, the lessons I learned stayed with me. Every day you are on the Kick-off team. You face obstacles, and you learn to solve problems and get-up when the outcome is not what you expected. This is essentially the essence of what I hope to share with you: the importance of being fully present, fully engaged, and always ready to show up.

02 No Excuses, Show Up

Your personal culture—your values, beliefs, and habits—is shaped by family, mentors, coaches, and experiences. It evolves through the decisions you make and the outcomes you encounter along the way. During my time as a cadet at the United States Military Academy at West Point, I had the privilege of being on the Strength Team under one of the best strength coaches in the country. His influence in the strength and conditioning field would extend far beyond West Point, for he later became the strength coach in the National Football League.

Working with our Strength Coach was far beyond strength and conditioning—it was about mastering discipline. Every movement had to be executed with precision, proper technique, and the right velocity. Success was measured through accountability: tracking sets, repetition, resistance, and progress. The lessons weren't just about getting stronger—they were about showing up, doing the work, and building a foundation of discipline.

Every day after class, my teammates and I would gather on the third floor of Arvin Gymnasium, where the Strength Coach gave us our instructions. Working with West Point athletes on the Nautilus workout program was educational, a phenomenal experience, and it was a chance to have a positive impact on others, to absorb the fundamentals of strength training, and to forge lifelong friendships with teammates. Those daily interactions were powerful, teaching me the value of camaraderie and personal growth through shared experiences.

Lessons in Discipline: From West Point to the 101st Airborne Division

After graduating from West Point and completing the Officer Basic Course at Fort Bliss in Texas, I was assigned to the 1/3 ADA Battalion in the 101st Airborne Division at Fort Campbell, Kentucky. Every day in the 101st began the same way: at 0630 sharp, over 12,000 soldiers gathered for physical training. Before any physical training, the chain of command would take accountability. You were expected to Show Up—on time, in the correct uniform, and with the right mindset to train hard.

> THE COMMON THREAD BETWEEN MY EXPERIENCES WITH THE STRENGTH TEAM AT WEST POINT AND PHYSICAL TRAINING IN THE 101ST WAS CLEAR: DISCIPLINE. IT WAS ABOUT SHOWING-UP—BEING FULLY PRESENT, MENTALLY AND PHYSICALLY PREPARED TO PUSH YOURSELF TO THE LIMIT, SURROUNDED BY OTHERS WHO SHARED THAT SAME MINDSET.

I've always believed that working out of the home is not the best solution. Sure, home fitness equipment starts off with good intentions, but how often does that treadmill become a glorified clothes rack? True progress happens when you're in a gym, with others who challenge and inspire you. Whether it's weight loss, aerobic and strength conditioning, you need to Show Up—fully engaged and ready to work. That same principle applies to every aspect of life.

Show Up in Business, Too

Just as in fitness, showing up is essential in business. Whether you're working on a proposal, forecasting finances, or brainstorming strategies, there's no substitute for being physically and mentally engaged. How often do you stumble upon a breakthrough idea in a hallway conversation or the office coffee room? Collaboration—true problem-solving—happens when people are present, sharing insights, and asking questions.

Risk assessment is another area where showing up matters. People approach risk differently based on their experience, but understanding and mitigating risk requires focused, in-depth discussions. You can't grasp the "Paul Harvey"—the rest of the story—without being fully immersed. The best solutions come from gathering the right people in a room, isolating the issue, analyzing risks, and exploring courses of action together.

Preparation: The Backbone of Showing Up

Discipline and preparation go hand-in-hand. I've always valued preparation, whether through handwritten notes or digital tools.

Capturing major points, jotting down questions, and thinking through potential challenges before a meeting sets you up for success. I call this "Prepare on Paper" (PoP)—the deliberate effort to plan, strategize, and rehearse before engaging in any interaction. Showing up is physical presence and being mentally ready. Too often, people attend meetings unprepared, generating questions on the fly and reacting instead of contributing meaningfully. Poor preparation leads to follow-up meetings that could have been avoided with better planning from the start.

How often do we hear people say they're overwhelmed with back-to-back meetings? It's become standard procedure. But without time set aside to think, plan, and prepare, those meetings become unproductive. To show up effectively, you should block off 1.5 times the length of the meeting on your calendar for preparation. The actual amount of time may vary based upon the complexity of the subject matter and the knowledge acquired beforehand. That prep time should be non-negotiable, as critical as the meeting itself.

PoP ensures that when you show up, you're ready to contribute. It transforms you from a passive observer to an active participant, someone who drives discussions forward rather than reacting to them. Meetings without PoP often lead to confusion, miscommunication, and essentially wasted time. With PoP, you provide clarity to issues, challenges and decisions.

Avoid Being a Mannequin in the Room

Showing up means more than occupying a chair in a meeting or clicking "Join" on a virtual call. I've seen too many people drift into meetings unprepared—what I call "mannequins." A mannequin might be physically present, but they aren't engaged. Even in virtual settings, a mannequin's only contribution might be sending an emoji or a reaction—hardly a substitute for real participation.

> TRUE ENGAGEMENT REQUIRES MORE THAN ATTENDANCE. IT REQUIRES PREPARATION, CRITICAL THINKING, AND ACTIVE INVOLVEMENT.

A mannequin adds no value to a discussion, while someone who shows up prepared can shape outcomes and drive progress. Whether in the gym, the office, or a virtual meeting, showing up—mentally and physically—is what makes the difference.

03 Show Up in a Hybrid Environment

Since the COVID-19 pandemic, the hybrid workforce has become the new normal. There are countless variations based on job functions, security requirements, time zones, and performance expectations. And with that shift has come a new debate—what exactly does it mean to "be at work"? For some, having headphones in while grocery shopping or cutting the grass seems to count as billable time. But here's the truth: Being connected is not the same as Showing Up.

While physical presence will always trump remote work, many companies have adopted hybrid models that are here to stay. Personally, I'm not a fan of hybrid work, but I understand that this is the direction many businesses have chosen, and that some employees actively seek out roles with hybrid options. The challenge lies in making hybrid work effective—and that means showing up in every sense of the word.

Redefining What Work Really Means

In a hybrid environment, it's critical to define what qualifies as work. Walking through a grocery store with an earbud in and your phone tucked into your pocket isn't working. Real work requires focus—thinking critically, analyzing data, coordinating actions, and solving problems.

Being logged in doesn't mean you're productive; true productivity comes from being mentally present and actively engaged.

A key part of making hybrid work successful is clarifying expectations. Employees should block off meeting preparation time on their calendars, just as they would for any other task. Clear triggers should be established for reporting key events—what the military calls Commander's Critical Information Requirements (CCIRs). In the business world, CCIRs could include events related to finance, human resources, IT, cybersecurity, operations, and safety.

For every critical development—whether positive or negative—the organization must be ready to act. Using a simple 5W structure (Who, What, When, Where, Why) ensures concise and timely communication. The first 5W report on any incident is labeled "First Report." The 5W provides an overview, and follow-up reports, tagged with date and time, keeps everyone updated as the situation evolves. Clear communication like this is essential for problem solving, efficient and effective operations, whether remote or in-person.

Preparation Is Key: Preparing on Paper (PoP)

To succeed in a hybrid world, preparation becomes even more important. While face-to-face meetings foster spontaneous collaboration, much of the groundwork can—and should—be laid remotely.

> PREPARING ON PAPER (POP) MEANS TAKING THE TIME TO FRAME THE PROBLEM, THINK THROUGH YOUR QUESTIONS, AND REHEARSE YOUR CONTRIBUTIONS BEFORE THE MEETING BEGINS.

It's about translating information into understanding—and then into knowledge.

The importance of preparation was reinforced during my time in the Army. I served under General McKiernan who transformed the traditional Battlefield Update Brief (BUB) into what he called the Battlefield Update Assessment (BUA). The difference? The BUA was not about regurgitating information—it was about providing insight, offering analysis, and assessing second- and third-order impacts.

This approach applies to any organization. Whether in-person or virtual, meetings should go beyond sharing information—they should highlight risk, options, and a desired action. Showing up prepared means understanding not just what happened, but what will happen next and how it affects the bigger picture.

The Art of Saying No

A critical lesson I've learned from decades of military and business experience is the value of "knowing when to say no". I once attended a presentation at the headquarters of a fast-food chain. Afterward, I asked the CEO why they didn't serve breakfast. For 15 minutes, he walked me through the thoughtful analysis behind that decision. It was absolutely masterful—understanding when an idea, no matter how tempting, isn't the right path to pursue.

Years later, the company introduced breakfast under new leadership. Every time I pass one of their locations in the morning, I notice the empty drive-thru lanes. The lesson? Bold decisions aren't just about saying Yes—they're also about knowing when to say No. And that clarity only comes from experience, preparation, and engagement—in other words, from showing up.

Rehearse, Rehearse, Rehearse

In a remote setting, preparation isn't enough—you also need to rehearse. Practicing your talking points, ensuring your slides work smoothly, and familiarizing yourself with virtual tools are essential for delivering a polished presentation. Too often, people assume they can wing it in virtual meetings, leading to technical hiccups and wasted time.

Block off preparation time on your calendar and use it wisely. Rehearsal ensures that when the meeting starts, you're not fumbling with technology—you're focused on delivering value. Showing up is about more than logging in on time; it's about setting the conditions to create positive outcomes.

Maintaining "Walk-Around Leadership" in a Virtual World

One thing you lose in a hybrid environment is the ability to practice "walk-around leadership." In an office, leaders can get a sense of how the team is doing just by walking through the workspace. That kind of informal check-in builds trust and offers valuable insights. In a remote world, it takes a little more effort.

I recommend scheduling 10-15 minute pulse-check calls with each member of your team. Other words one-on-one calls. These conversations don't always need to be about work—they can be social or a mix of both. The goal is to stay connected, demonstrate that you care, and gather insights you might not get in a formal meeting. Back-to-back meetings are not a badge of honor; real leadership happens between those meetings; in the time you invest building relationships and staying engaged.

The Face Behind the Screen Matters

In virtual meetings, your presence is about being visible. Cameras on sends a clear message: "I am here, engaged, and ready to contribute." When participants hide behind blank screens, it suggests they're multitasking, distracted, or not fully invested. And let's be honest—multitasking doesn't work. Just like that dusty home treadmill, it's an illusion of productivity.

When you show up in a hybrid environment, your focus matters. Your preparation, presence, and engagement set the tone for the rest of the team. Whether you're leading a meeting or participating, showing up means being all in—mentally, physically, and emotionally.

IN THE

FIGHT

04 **The Arena**

When I first stepped into West Point in the summer of 1976, it was like nothing I'd ever experienced. Being away from home was a shock, but what hit even harder was the intensity of Beast Barracks, a six-week summer program designed to push New Cadets to our limits, mentally and physically. I don't recall every detail of those grueling weeks, but one thing stands out clearly: being introduced to "The Man in the Arena"—a powerful passage from Theodore Roosevelt's speech "Citizenship in a Republic," given at the Sorbonne in Paris in 1910. We had to memorize it and recite a portion of his speech word for word, at the position of attention and without a single mistake.

"IT IS NOT THE CRITIC WHO COUNTS; NOT THE MAN WHO POINTS OUT HOW THE STRONG MAN STUMBLES OR WHERE THE DOER OF DEEDS COULD HAVE DONE THEM BETTER. THE CREDIT BELONGS TO THE MAN WHO IS ACTUALLY IN THE ARENA, WHOSE FACE IS MARRED BY DUST AND SWEAT AND BLOOD; WHO STRIVES VALIANTLY; WHO ERRS, WHO COMES SHORT AGAIN AND AGAIN, BECAUSE THERE IS NO EFFORT WITHOUT ERROR AND SHORTCOMING; BUT WHO DOES ACTUALLY STRIVE TO DO THE DEEDS; WHO KNOWS GREAT ENTHUSIASMS, THE GREAT DEVOTIONS; WHO SPENDS HIMSELF IN A WORTHY CAUSE; WHO AT THE BEST KNOWS IN THE END THE TRIUMPH OF HIGH ACHIEVEMENT, AND WHO AT THE WORST, IF HE FAILS, AT LEAST FAILS WHILE DARING GREATLY, SO THAT HIS PLACE SHALL NEVER BE WITH THOSE COLD AND TIMID SOULS WHO NEITHER KNOW VICTORY NOR DEFEAT."

~ THEODORE ROOSEVELT

After graduating from West Point, I kept a copy of that passage in a plastic frame, and for more than three decades, it had a place in my office or home. The speech encapsulated a core aspect of my personal culture, becoming a constant reminder to lead by showing up and being in the arena, alongside those facing the real challenges—not sitting in the cheap seats, where it's easy to criticize and point fingers.

Being in the Arena in Business

In the world of federal service contracts, the stakes are high. We often bid on contracts in complex and dangerous locations, from Iraq to Afghanistan. One crucial question always came up: If we win this contract, will our corporate leaders visit the employees on the ground? If the answer was no, then why were we even bidding? Our CEO made it a point to visit employees no matter where they were or what conditions they faced. That willingness to show up in the harshest environments wasn't just symbolic; it built respect, loyalty, and a sense of unity. It was a clear message: We're in this together.

This, I believe, is showing up in its purest form. When leaders are willing to step into the arena alongside their teams, it fosters camaraderie, a shared commitment, and an unmatched passion for the mission.

The After Action Review (AAR): Learning from Experience

In the Army, we used the After Action Review (AAR) as a routine, structured approach to analyze each mission or exercise. After every deployment, training, or operation, we would conduct an AAR to answer three core questions: What happened? What should have happened? And what can we do better next time?

The goal of an AAR is straightforward—to pinpoint strengths, identify areas for improvement, and make sure we're better prepared for the future. This isn't about finding someone to blame but about gaining insight and preparing for the next challenge. The focus is always on learning and progressing as a team.

Success and failure both have their lessons, and the AAR provided a clear path forward. It was a way to keep everyone in the arena, fully engaged and ready to act on what we learned. To participate in an AAR, you had to show up—you couldn't be in the stands or somewhere on the sidelines. This commitment to continuous improvement echoed Roosevelt's words louder than ever.

The Corporate Arena: Showing Up at Work

After retiring from the military, I transitioned to the defense industry, where the mission was to provide products and/or services to meet the needs of federal agencies. We'd receive requests for proposals from various agencies, and our company would submit solutions that provided expertise, technology, and innovations to meet mission requirements. The entire process could span one to two years, requiring relentless dedication, teamwork, and expertise.

When we won a contract, there were celebrations all around—high-fives, smiles, and "win parties." But when we lost, the atmosphere was tense.

Losing brought real consequences: budget cuts, revisiting strategy, and potentially restructuring.

This was the reality of being in the business arena. To truly succeed, you have to show up—win or lose, rain or shine.

But when losses occurred, there was a critical need to understand why. Finger-pointing from the sidelines was all too common. Yet, in an environment focused on showing up, that energy was redirected. Instead of blaming, we aimed to bring everyone into the arena.

We tackled this by having all key leaders read each proposal and then we would all huddle for an intense, uninterrupted 48-hour review session. For those two days, everyone was part of the process, immersed in content, format, and attention to detail. We left no room for finger-pointing. Success and failure were shared, and the outcome was a stronger, more unified team—one that understood the value of showing up together.

The Power of an AAR in Business

Bringing the AAR methodology into the corporate world proved invaluable. It wasn't just a military procedure; it was a powerful tool for improvement. By openly discussing what went wrong and brainstorming how to improve, we fostered a learning environment that strengthened the entire organization. In a climate where people often walk on eggshells to avoid blame, the AAR provided a constructive way to address challenges and drive improvement.

> THE BEAUTY OF AN AAR IS THAT IT MOVES FINGER-POINTERS INTO THE ARENA. IT ENERGIZES THE ORGANIZATION, ENABLING EVERYONE TO TAKE OWNERSHIP OF BOTH SUCCESSES AND FAILURES.

When victory comes, the shared sense of accomplishment is profound. The company understands that showing up isn't just a slogan; it's a vital part of the organizational culture.

Building an Arena-Minded Team

When you ensure that everyone involved understands expectations, shares in the planning, and is open to honest feedback, you set the stage for success. Roosevelt's words ring true: "The credit belongs to the man who is actually in the arena." Being in the arena isn't about sitting in the stands watching from afar; it's about being on the ground, in the midst of the action, fully immersed.

Creating an arena-minded team means everyone shows up, prepared and ready to contribute. With a well-thought-out Prepare on Paper (PoP), clear guidance, and a shared commitment to the mission, you turn a collection of individuals into a unified, powerful force. That's the essence of Showing Up—it's not just about being there; it's about being all in.

05 Perseverance and Resiliency—Your Body Armor

Again, every day, you're on the kick-off team. You're lined up, helmet on, pads in place—your "gear" made up of your education, experience, and exposure. As you move down the field, obstacles appear. You quickly realize not everything will be easy, and sometimes, you'll get knocked down—physically, mentally, or both. You might find yourself flat on your back, staring up at the sky, exhausted and confused. This football analogy captures two essential qualities of showing up: perseverance and resiliency.

When you show up, you come ready, both mentally and physically. You're prepared because, in the arena, there will be times when you don't succeed. Losses build experience, and from that experience, you gain the resilience and perseverance to keep going. An After Action Review (AAR) helps you break down what happened, what should have happened and how to improve. And then, armed with those insights, you get back in the fight, ready to tackle the next mission with renewed purpose.

Being in the arena guarantees you'll face obstacles head-on, and sometimes, you'll stumble. But you're not sitting in the cheap seats, pointing fingers at those taking risks.

> TRUE RESILIENCE AND PERSEVERANCE GROW ONLY FROM DIRECT EXPERIENCE IN THE ARENA.

In today's world, it often seems we give up too easily; bouncing back has become rare. But if you want to build a personal culture equipped for long-term success, resilience and perseverance become your body armor.

Building Strength Through the Fight

As you navigate obstacles, your problem-solving improves, your preparation strengthens, and your teamwork deepens. A few victories give you the confidence to take calculated risks and to act with boldness. When the dust settles, you've created a personal culture that doesn't quit—a culture that gets back up after every fall. But the first step is always the same: you have to show up, fully prepared, mentally and physically, to meet the challenges in the arena.

Perseverance and Resiliency: Essential Body Armor

Resilience and perseverance are your body armor as you fight in the arena. Those who wear this armor with pride are the teammates you want by your side—the ones who show up and stand strong, no matter the challenge. These are the people who represent the best of any organization. They know what it means to keep going, to get back up after every setback, and to keep pushing forward.

> IN THE END, THIS BODY ARMOR ISN'T JUST PROTECTION; IT'S A MINDSET THAT FUELS YOU TO SHOW UP DAY AFTER DAY, READY TO FACE WHATEVER COMES NEXT.

06 Show Up Together—Teamwork

Teamwork. You truly understand its value when you have experience or exposure to being assigned to a work group, a team, or an organization that supports a common purpose. You develop skills, workable procedures, and the right mindset when you are on a team. That's why I believe every kid should play a sport. Growing up in the Anderson household, I didn't get to pick; I was expected to play baseball, football, and basketball. Each season, I was on a team. I'm sure If I didn't make the school team, I would have joined the YMCA or found another organization. It wasn't up for discussion: I was expected to play, play well, and improve over the season. Sports teach you many things, but nothing as valuable as teamwork.

Playing on a team with others, each with their own strengths and weaknesses, teaches you resilience. You learn who has a strong skill sets and who struggles—and it doesn't really matter which category you fall into. What matters is that as a team, you're all focused on one thing: accomplishing the desired outcome. And when you don't, the team works together to assess what went wrong, and how they can prevent that same outcome from happening again. Being better the next time is the overarching goal.

Bouncing back from a loss or rallying from a slow start to win are two golden lessons that will serve you for life. Those scenarios demand the kind of mental and physical focus that strengthens you and the team as the season goes on. You learn perseverance and resiliency—and you learn to work as a team. A team isn't a fixed thing; sometimes it changes, and so does each player's role. The coach or senior leader is there to make sure everyone's in the right place, ensuring the team is as ready as possible. If one area is weak, adjustments are made. You learn quickly that the team's success is a product of collective talent.

As a team, you don't quit. After every setback, you ask: what happened, what should have happened, and what can we do to improve? Teams conduct After Action Reviews (AARs) to grow stronger and avoid repeating mistakes. The lessons of resilience, bouncing back, and getting better apply to every part of life—whether at work, in sports, as a parent, or any role you take on.

Learning Together, Winning Together

Learning to work with others toward a common goal is one of life's greatest lessons. You can't put a price tag on the value of that experience. When a team comes together, every individual grows. Resilience and perseverance flourish, building confidence as each player feels ownership in both wins and losses.

> BUT LIKE ALL THINGS IN LIFE, YOU AND THE TEAM MUST SHOW UP. TOGETHER. YOU CAN'T BE A TEAM WHEN SOME ARE IN THE ARENA, AND OTHERS ARE WATCHING FROM THE CHEAP SEATS.

True teamwork demands everyone's presence, accountability, and shared purpose.

In the end, nothing replaces the power of being together, face-to-face, with a common goal. No software or remote tool can replace the value of showing up together as a team.

GEAR UP
AND GO

07 Spartans—A Must-Have in the Arena

As a young lieutenant, I started using the term "Spartan" to describe someone you could count on—someone with discipline, resilience, and an unshakable drive to get the job done. Just like the legendary warriors of ancient Greece, these people were skilled, fierce, and steadfast under pressure.

> A SPARTAN IS SOMEONE WHO DOESN'T QUIT, WHO PUSHES THROUGH THE CHALLENGES, AND WHO SETS A STANDARD OTHERS WANT TO FOLLOW.

A Spartan produces consistent performance. In the military, workplace, or sports team, a Spartan is the teammate you want by your side.

In every organization, no matter its size, people are the key. Strategies, plans, and missions all depend on having the right people in the right places. Finding Spartans for your team isn't easy, but it's a journey you must invest time and energy in order to be successful. As a leader, you have to Show Up prepared, understanding your organization, knowing what qualities you need to solve problems and drive growth. Landing a Spartan is a team effort.

Identifying and Leveraging the Spartans in Your Organization

Every organization has a handful of Spartans. They're the people who are fully engaged 24/7, who think critically and creatively to solve problems, and who bring others along with them. They are resilient, focused, and keep the team moving in the right direction. But here's a key point: Use your Spartans to drive opportunities, not to fix problems.

Spartans aren't always the loudest in the room or those in the limelight; sometimes, they're behind the scenes, quietly making sure things run smoothly. They show up every day, committed and consistent, but they may go unnoticed by senior leaders. It's your job as a leader to recognize these invisible warriors, the ones who get things done right the first time. Find them, value them, and make sure they stay on your team.

How to Recognize a Spartan

A Spartan stands out through their habits and discipline. They're the ones carrying a notebook, taking notes, making plans, and preparing action steps to tackle challenges and capture opportunities. They keep you informed, they know the market and the customer, and they understand the product. A Spartan doesn't just perform—they do their homework, operate on both tactical and strategic levels, and ask insightful questions.

To keep a Spartan on your team, strong leadership is essential. Compensation matters, of course, but who they report to is even more important.

> **SPARTANS THRIVE UNDER LEADERS WHO HAVE THREE KEY QUALITIES:**
>
> 1. **HUMILITY** – HUMBLE LEADERS DON'T NECESSARILY THINK LESS OF THEMSELVES, BUT THEY DO THINK OF THEMSELVES LESS. HUMBLE LEADERS ARE FOCUSED ON THE TEAM, NOT JUST THEMSELVES.
> 2. **RESPONSIBILITY** – TRUE LEADERS TAKE RESPONSIBILITY RATHER THAN POINTING FINGERS. THEY OWN THEIR DECISIONS, POLICIES, AND GUIDANCE.
> 3. **PRESENCE** – SPARTANS EXPECT THEIR LEADERS TO BE IN THE ARENA WITH THEM, FULLY ENGAGED AND SHOWING UP ALONGSIDE THEM.

With the right leadership, Spartans will stay on your team, providing consistent results and setting a high standard of excellence.

Keeping Spartans on the Bus

You won't have many Spartans, so make sure you give them the guidance they need and empower them to accomplish critical tasks that drive your organization's vision forward. Their feedback on strategy is invaluable, and their focus, resilience, and ability to tackle challenges head-on can lift an organization to new heights. But most importantly, Spartans respond to good leadership. When they feel valued and supported, they deliver extraordinary results.

When You Don't Have Any Spartans

What if, after eight to twelve months, you realize there are no Spartans on your team? You might not notice this unless you're actively present, engaged, and showing up. If you find yourself without Spartans, it's time to consider making some changes. Finding the right Spartan is no small task. It requires knowing your organization's needs, identifying the right fit, and conducting thorough interviews. Define the attributes, skills, and personality you're looking for, and develop interview questions to reveal those qualities.

The Power of a Few Spartans

Every organization needs at least a few Spartans. While an entire company filled with them might sound ideal, it's not realistic. The strength and continuity of any organization—whether a business, a military unit, or a family—depend on having Spartans in the mix. Keep them on the bus, give them room to grow, and watch your organization thrive.

08 **No Moonwalking–Problem Solving**

In many organizations, a common frustration is that management takes too long to make decisions. When delays drag on, people start assuming leadership simply doesn't care—and once that impression sets in, it's difficult to change. There's no doubt that morale in an organization is critical. But as always, the first step to addressing any issue is to Show Up.

If you're new to an organization or you've received feedback about low morale, it's essential to get in front of the group and start a discussion. Most of the time, you're working with a capable team that's ready to provide honest feedback. Sometimes, it helps to break a large group into smaller groups by function or rank, but whatever the organizational climate, the key is to move forward deliberately. No moonwalking—just progress.

The 3x5 Card Drill

For over 40 years, one of my go-to techniques for gathering honest feedback has been the 3x5 card drill. This method is simple, anonymous, and highly effective. Here's how it works: after a brief discussion of the organization's vision and current strategy, I hand out a 3x5 card and a pen to each person. On one side, they place a positive sign (+) and write down three things they appreciate about the organization. On the other side, they place a negative sign (-) and jot down three things they feel could be improved. No names, no extra details—just three positives and three negatives.

Once everyone's done, I collect the cards and bring them back to my office. Over the weekend, I sort through each card and record the comments on two sheets of paper: one for the positives and one for the negatives. Each time the same feedback appears, I add a tick mark next to it. This creates a frequency diagram that highlights the most common sentiments.

Prioritizing and Addressing Feedback

Once all the feedback is organized, it's time to identify and prioritize the top three positive and negative comments with the highest frequency. For the top three negatives, the goal is to determine if each one has a short-term or a long-term fix. The issues with the most frequency are the ones that matter most to your team, and it's essential to address them with clarity and purpose.

If an item can be fixed within a month, it goes straight onto the task list. In some cases, forming a small working group to build consensus can be effective. Long-term issues, on the other hand, might require a more comprehensive approach, regular working group meetings, and resource allocation. These issues often touch on company culture or significant changes like benefits, product adjustments, or work location policies, and tackling them requires tactical patience.

Visible Action Creates a Positive Environment

Taking quick, visible action and involving the team in problem-solving fosters a positive, engaged environment. When leadership shows up and takes action on employee feedback, it signals that they're serious about making improvements. They're not moonwalking, avoiding conflict, or delaying decisions—they're actively addressing the issues raised.

In the end, employees need to see that leadership isn't hiding in their offices but is genuinely committed to solving problems. When you show up, listen, and respond to the issues your team has raised, morale improves, performance strengthens, and attrition drops. This is when leadership truly shows up.

09 Mastering the Basics—A Product of Showing Up

Showing up means being present, both mentally and physically. There's nothing more valuable than arriving prepared, with the confidence that comes from knowing you've done the groundwork. As you navigate life's "obstacle course," you come to realize that you can only coach, mentor, or lead up to the limit of your own abilities. Your effectiveness is shaped by your experience, education and exposure—no magic shortcuts here!

The more you follow Rule #1 show up, the more you'll grow. Showing up allows you to observe what works, what doesn't, and to ask questions that deepen your knowledge. To get the most out of each opportunity, preparation is essential. Jot down questions in your notebook, do your research, and get some context before you walk into a meeting or site visit.

During a site visit, these questions will help you identify "what right looks like." The experts will share their insights, regulations, standards, and options, and you'll be there, absorbing everything, taking notes, asking questions, and sharpening your perspective. Mastering the fundamentals of any job or sport builds the foundation for success and often sets you apart from others. Learning never stops, and being your best each day is a continual process. You can only teach, coach, or mentor others effectively when you've mastered the basics yourself. This "blocking and tackling" is what makes you a valuable asset to any organization—and maybe even a Spartan.

Knowing What Right Looks Like

The power of knowing what right looks like lies in the basics. After years in the military and as a contractor in the Federal Service Industry, I can walk into a warehouse, motor pool, or welding shop, ask for a few records, and immediately spot areas that need work. This skill didn't come from guesswork; it's the result of showing up and learning firsthand.

When you've logged the hours and have the education, experience, and exposure you start to see things others miss. I've watched seasoned experts unpack issues with laser-sharp questions that cut to the heart of the matter. They've shown up repeatedly, and through years of doing so, they've built a store of knowledge and a clear vision of what right looks like. They know the standards and can spot even the smallest shortfall.

This insight is critical, especially for young leaders. I've seen them walk past safety violations simply because they didn't recognize them. Coaching others on what right looks like is essential to an organization's future, and it's up to those with the knowledge to pass it on. That's where a few Spartans come in, ready to coach and mentor others, so they, too, can learn to recognize and uphold the standard. Knowing the standard, and having the courage to correct issues, creates a thriving environment of continuous improvement.

In the Field: Pre-Combat Checks and Knowing What's Essential

I remember being at the line of departure before the U.S. crossed into Iraq. The air war had begun, and ground forces prepared to move, with close air support and long-range fire ready to launch. I saw leaders up and down the line conducting pre-combat checks, going over every vehicle, asking combat crews questions about mission objectives, equipment, and supply readiness. These leaders knew what right looked like, and they weren't leaving anything to chance. They ensured every detail was checked, every supply accounted for, and every weapon prepared.

I recall watching leaders ask to see their ammunition, first aid kit, food/water, protective gear, and communication devices.

> PRE-COMBAT CHECKS, DONE RIGHT, SAVE LIVES AND IMPACT MISSION OUTCOMES. IT'S NO DIFFERENT IN DAILY LIFE: WHETHER IT'S A VACATION, A SCHOOL RUN, OR A MAJOR PURCHASE, BEING READY, ASKING THE RIGHT QUESTIONS, AND DOING YOUR DUE DILIGENCE MEANS YOU'RE SHOWING UP FOR SUCCESS.

The Basics are Non-Negotiable

If you show me a work environment with frequent accidents, I'll show you an organization missing a few Spartans. Neglecting the basics leads to failure. Early in my Army career, I commanded a unit with sophisticated radar and weapons systems designed to track, identify, and engage enemy threats. On Day 1, I emphasized three simple but crucial principles—our "blocking and tackling" for mission success:

1. Physical Fitness – We focused on building strength, endurance, and readiness for each soldier.

2. Preventative Maintenance – Every soldier was certified and trained to keep equipment fully operational, always ready for action.

3. Marksmanship – We set the goal that every soldier should qualify as an expert in the weapon they are assigned to carry in combat.

With detailed programs and oversight, we turned these three areas into the bedrock of our unit. And the impact went beyond these basics; the attention to detail spread to all our training and operations. When you master the basics, everything else falls into place.

The Basics in Business

In one of the companies I led, we focused on three core areas: Lean Six Sigma, Capture Management, and On-Contract Performance. Mastering these basics created a culture where every contract was executed above standard, workplace safety was prioritized, and revenue and profit grew consistently. Whether in the military,

business, or sports, focusing on the fundamentals drives consistency in extraordinary performance. Mastering the basics builds a team that thrives together in the arena.

No matter the environment—consistently Showing Up and mastering the basics is the recipe for success. It's where the foundation of excellence is laid, and it's here, in the fundamentals, that you truly show up.

INTO THE

ARENA

10   Family and Friends

Anytime you sit down with someone over 70, the conversation often drifts to a common theme: "time flies by." I've heard it countless times since I was a kid, and it's more than just an observation—it's a universal truth. On Monday you blink, and suddenly it's Friday! Life speeds by, and the challenge is figuring out how to slow it down, to be fully present in the moments that matter. Some find this in fishing, tossing a baseball with their kids, mowing the lawn, or taking a quiet walk with their spouse. Whatever the approach, the question remains: how do you slow the train down and truly enjoy life?

> HAPPINESS IS A UNIVERSAL PURSUIT, BUT EVERYONE'S PATH TO IT LOOKS DIFFERENT. AT ITS CORE, HAPPINESS OFTEN REVOLVES AROUND ONE THING: RELATIONSHIPS—FAMILY AND FRIENDS.

We live in a world where families and friends are increasingly scattered. After high school, many people leave home for jobs, college, or trade school, and life takes them far from their roots. Friendships forged in youth face the strain of distance and time. In this reality, staying connected means showing up.

Reunions—whether family gatherings, high school get-togethers, or long-overdue visits—are moments you shouldn't miss. We don't all have unlimited travel budgets or endless vacation days, but if you prioritize anything, let it be these reunions. Reconnecting with family and friends, reliving shared memories, and reinforcing those bonds are some of life's greatest joys. You never quite grasp their importance until you're there, seeing old friends and loved ones. Showing up in times like these rekindles relationships that might otherwise fade. And it's the same when someone close to you faces hardship, celebrates a marriage, or goes through a major life event. You show up.

Don't Let a Big House Hold You Back

I've always believed that your home shouldn't consume a disproportionate amount of your income. The biggest barrier to showing up can be a Big Ass House (BAH)—a mortgage, insurance, and taxes that leave little for anything else. When your family and friends are spread across the country, the cost of travel and lodging can add up. But happiness isn't about "stuff." True happiness is found in the presence of family and friends, and avoiding unnecessary financial strain opens the door to these moments. When you choose showing up over material things, it's an investment in memories that will last a lifetime.

Parents as Inflection Points

Parents are the first inflection points in a child's life. They shape young people through the values they instill, the sacrifices they make, and, perhaps most importantly, by simply being there. While friends, coaches, and teachers all have their influence, Mom and Dad are at the point of the spear.

If I had to name one defining attribute of my parents, it would be this: they showed up. At every parent-teacher conference, they were both present. They attended every game of every sport I played. My dad even came to every high school football practice, offering feedback over dinner.

When I went to West Point, he visited regularly to check on how I was handling the rigorous environment. During my second year, when I was considering leaving before my active-duty commitment kicked in, he drove over 10 hours from Kentucky to talk me into staying. It was a short conversation—less than an hour—and then he was back on the road. But that conversation changed my life, steering me toward a 32-year career in service to our country. Moments like these are life-altering inflection points, and they don't happen unless you show up. My Dad showed-up.

My mom and dad attended every promotion ceremony throughout my Army career. No location was too far—they saved, set aside vacation time, and put the family above all else to be there. They sacrificed Christmas gifts, new cars, and career advancements to show up for their kids. My dad wasn't focused on climbing the ladder but on staying at a level where he could prioritize us. His philosophy was simple: show up.

11 Plate Spinners vs. Ball Jugglers

I remember watching late-night TV in the 1970s—a rare treat since it was usually past my bedtime. These shows revolved around a charismatic host performing comedy routines and chatting with celebrities, but what stuck with me wasn't the jokes or the interviews. It was the performers they brought on stage, specifically the jugglers.

I didn't expect to see jugglers outside a circus, so watching them on TV felt extraordinary. The first time, it was a classic ball juggler. He skillfully tossed and caught four balls—larger than baseballs—effortlessly maintaining their rhythm in midair. His movements were precise, his timing impeccable, and his concentration unshakable.

The second time, it was a plate spinner. This performance was entirely different. The plate spinner's task was to balance and spin ceramic plates on tall sticks. One by one, he got the plates spinning and then moved quickly from stick to stick to keep them rotating. It was mesmerizing to watch him manage up to a dozen spinning plates at once, darting back and forth to ensure none of them crashed to the floor.

Both performances were impressive displays of agility, timing, and coordination. But the difference was striking: the ball juggler worked with four objects, while the plate spinner managed twelve. Even at a young age, I knew which one I aspired to emulate—not as an entertainer, but as a professional.

> WHATEVER PROFESSION I WAS TO PURSUE, I WANTED TO BE A PLATE SPINNER.

The Metaphor of the Plate Spinner

To me, each spinning plate represented a program, skill set, or responsibility. I didn't want to limit myself to juggling just a few tasks. I wanted to contribute more—to bring versatility, balance, and adaptability to any organization I joined. Plate spinners don't just keep things in motion; they excel at managing multiple processes, functions, and ensuring everything is moving forward.

In my military career, I focused on mastering the fundamentals from the bottom up. Maintenance, operations, planning, weapons, personnel, intelligence, communications—each one was a spinning plate that I learned to keep in motion. When I transitioned into business, the same principle applied. Whether it was managing HR, finance, safety, security, and quality or various projects, developing strategies, or solving complex problems, I approached my work as a plate spinner.

The Power of the Plate Spinner

This isn't multitasking, where attention is scattered across several things at once. Plate spinning is about giving focused attention to one task, mastering it, and then moving on to the next while ensuring the first plate keeps spinning. It's a discipline of balance, precision, and follow-through.

The Army's Non-Commissioned Officers (NCOs) are some of the finest examples of plate spinners. They manage a wide range of duties, skills, and responsibilities while leading their teams toward a common purpose. Imagine if all NCOs were ball jugglers, handling only a few tasks at a time! The Army would need twice the personnel to accomplish the same missions. Plate spinners multiply the effectiveness of their teams and organizations.

Plate Spinners in Action

When I was looking to build a strong team, I sought out plate spinners—people who had mastered the skills needed to handle complex tasks. These individuals often became the Spartans of the organization, those who showed up, made an impact, and could handle the demands of cross-functional teams.

Ball jugglers, by contrast, are becoming less relevant in today's fast-paced, interconnected work environments. Specializing in one area is no longer enough. To be effective, you need to master multiple disciplines.

Every day, the question isn't just what you'll accomplish but how many plates you'll spin. Each plate represents a key function or task, while the stick it spins on is the process that drives it. Your job is to ensure all functional areas are executing to standard and in synch with other functions.

Becoming a Plate Spinner

The plate spinner's approach is to spin the plates, improve performance, and to keep operations going. It's a mindset that prioritizes mastery of the basics, adaptability in the face of challenges, and the perseverance to keep moving. Ask yourself: how many plates can I keep spinning today? Focus on each one, ensure it's spinning properly, and then move to the next.

In the end, plate spinners are the ones who make organizations thrive. They don't just juggle—they balance, manage, and lead with precision and intent. Be the plate spinner who shows up, takes on the challenge, and ensures that everything runs smoothly.

12 Show-Up and Stay

Showing up is your first step toward success—it's how you put your best foot forward. When you step into the arena, you arrive prepared, with your body armor on and your Spartan teammates by your side. But showing up isn't the finish line; it's the starting point. Once you're there, the next critical move is to stay engaged.

The Danger of Just Showing Up

I've seen it too many times: people show up, make their presence known, and then leave before the real work begins. While they technically showed up, their quick departure often raises questions. How long you stay matters. It's not just about putting in time; it's about the quality and impact of your presence.

Deciding how long to stay requires judgment. It depends on the complexity of the issue, the nature of the discussion, and who else is present. One thing is certain: if you show up just to be seen, you're not really showing up.

Walking in, shaking a few hands, and leaving isn't enough. True presence means staying long enough to contribute, ask questions, offer insights, and make a difference.

The Importance of Staying Engaged

Once you're in the arena, everyone notices—both those working alongside you and the spectators in the cheap seats. People pay attention to who shows up, how they engage, and how long they stay. When you remain engaged, asking thoughtful questions, sharing ideas, and contributing to solutions, you set a powerful example for others.

Staying isn't about clocking hours; it's about the lasting impact you make while you're there. When you show up, stay, and get involved, you demonstrate preparation, teamwork, resilience, and perseverance. Your behavior becomes a benchmark for others to follow.

Leading by Example

The younger workforce and military personnel watch leaders closely. They learn what leadership looks like by observing those at the tip of the spear. When they see leaders showing up, staying engaged, investing time and energy, and becoming part of the solution, they're learning a lesson they'll carry throughout their lives. Your willingness to stay shows them what it means to truly own your role in the arena.

> WHETHER IN THE WORKPLACE, THE MILITARY, OR YOUR PERSONAL LIFE, STAYING ISN'T JUST ABOUT PHYSICAL PRESENCE. IT'S ABOUT BEING MENTALLY AND EMOTIONALLY INVESTED IN THE OUTCOME. IT'S ABOUT LEAVING A MARK, CREATING VALUE, AND DEMONSTRATING WHAT IT MEANS TO SHOW UP AND STAY.

Owning Your Presence in the Arena

The choice is yours: you can show up, make an appearance, and leave—or you can show up and own it. When you stay and engage, you're doing more than just participating. You're making a statement that your presence matters, that you're committed to seeing things through, and that you're part of the solution.

Show up. Stay. Set the standard for others to follow. When you invest your time and energy fully, you're not just in the arena—you're leading it.

LEAD THE

WAY

13 Show-Up and Be Happy

There have been countless studies and research completed on Happiness in America. These studies have covered several decades of personal interviews, analysis, and research. Obviously, everybody desires to chase the opportunity, the material object, or a partnership whether marriage, family, friends, teammates, or business partners. Everyone is seeking the golden egg of happiness whether it has an intrinsic or extrinsic value or both.

Bottomline, is we all seek happiness. However, not everybody finds it which suggests we could be chasing the wrong golden egg. We could also be chasing happiness from a distance or remotely.

It seems we tend to receive personal positive feedback when we fully immerse ourselves. When we are embraced in the moment, optimizing the time, and engage as an individual or as a team we tend to experience a positive feeling. Over the course of a lifetime, you experience a wide range of successes and failures. When you invest in deliberate planning and programming across multiple functional elements you experience the challenges and opportunities both coupled with the investment of time, energy, and resources. That experience is incredibly valuable. This is full immersion.

Full immersion does not happen unless you Show-Up. When you Show-Up you have clearly optimized beforehand, and have become fully immersed. This all leads to happiness.

> HAPPINESS IS A RESULT OF PREPARATION, EXECUTION, AND BEING FULLY IMMERSED. THE INVESTMENT OF TIME, ENERGY, AND RESOURCES ALL AIMED AT A POSITIVE OUTCOME.

However, if you don't have the outcome you desired, the investment of resources and your personal appearance will still contribute to your happiness. Showing-Up generates intrinsic value regardless of the outcome. Showing-Up is the most important contributor to happiness. Showing Up as a product of being at the right place and time, fully prepared and engaged generates happiness.

You can go buy a new car and six months later it generates zero level of happiness. You can buy a new TV and after a few weeks it generates zero level of happiness. You Show-Up at your friend's wedding, a son or daughter's sports event, a graduation ceremony of a cousin, or at a remote site in business and you have refueled the most sought after emotion on the planet—Happiness.

Generating memories far exceeds buying "Stuff" when considering what makes you Happy. There is more……

The other attribute you build when you Show-Up is Trust. Trust is measured behavior where you do what you said you would do. When family members can count on you being present or a workforce on a remote site can guarantee others you will visit, you build the most important attribute on this planet—Trust.

> TRUST IS SOMETHING THAT TAKES MONTHS TO YEARS TO DEVELOP AND UNFORTUNATELY, YOU CAN LOSE IT OVERNIGHT.

Being a busy person and Showing Up, prepared and fully engaged, generates what I call Trust Points. If you get enough Trust Points it leads to Trust Insurance because overtime, there will be something you can't Show-Up. Regardless of the reason, you may not Show-Up whereas others were counting on you to be present, fully committed and engaged. If you have Trust Insurance, you get a second chance!

If you said you will show-up, and you do, you build trust. To be a person who others trust is powerful. When others trust you, they have deep respect for your character and your willingness to Show-Up.

In the course of a lifetime, having the attributes of trust and discipline makes you valuable to family, friends and significant others. To build those attributes in today's remote, digitally connected world requires you to make a drastic change in behavior. That change leads to the most sought-after yet complex emotion. To be happy, you Show-Up.

14 Show-Up Roadmap

Life moves fast, and no one gets an endless supply of time. Along the way, you encounter inflection points—moments that shift your trajectory. Ideally, these inflection points steer you toward a positive path, but regardless of where they lead, your journey is defined by the roadmap you create. That roadmap shapes your personal culture, the essence of who you are, how you treat others, how you solve problems, and what drives you to be better version of yourself today.

In countless classrooms and discussions, I've heard instructors emphasize the importance of having a vision. They'd ask, "Who do you want to be in five years?" Establishing a vision is essential—it's the picture you're working to create. But achieving that vision requires a strategy, the "how" behind the "what." It's not enough to dream about the future; you need a plan to get there.

However, the path to your vision isn't built in five-year increments. It starts with showing up and doing your best today. If you don't give your all in the present, you may never reach the future you envision. As a young Second Lieutenant in the Army, I wasn't focused on becoming a General Officer; my priority was to be the best Second

Lieutenant I could be. Over time, my roadmap revealed itself, one step at a time.

This book has explored the principles of Showing Up, highlighting how it helps you develop a personal culture grounded in perseverance, resilience, and engagement. These principles can be distilled into a simple but powerful framework I call The Big Eight—a roadmap for showing up and becoming your best self.

> THE BIG EIGHT
> 1. PREPARE ON PAPER (POP) AND REHEARSE, AND REHEARSE AGAIN
> 2. GET IN THE ARENA
> 3. BE A SPARTAN
> 4. KNOW WHAT RIGHT LOOKS LIKE
> 5. WEAR YOUR BODY ARMOR: PERSEVERANCE AND RESILIENCY
> 6. SQUINT WITH YOUR EARS
> 7. PUSH DOWN SUCCESS
> 8. BUILD RELATIONSHIPS

1. Prepare on Paper and Rehearse

Showing up begins long before you step into the room. It starts with preparation. Write down your questions, ideas, and thoughts—don't rely on memory alone. Preparing on Paper stimulates thought and focus ensuring your delivery is clear, concise, and on-target. Whether in-person or virtual, preparation shows respect for others' time and signals that you're ready to engage.

In today's hybrid work environment, this preparation is more critical than ever. Without it, meetings lack focus and often require follow-ups that could have been avoided. Good preparation reduces the need for endless meetings and ensures productive outcomes.

2. Get in the Arena

To make an impact, you must leave the sidelines and step into the arena. Being in the arena means taking responsibility, being present, and staying engaged. Whether you win or lose, the experience makes you better. Finger-pointing has no place here—the only direction to point is at yourself.

3. Be a Spartan

Spartans are plate-spinners, skilled and versatile individuals who tackle complex tasks with focus and precision. They thrive in dynamic environments and contribute meaningfully to the team's mission. Spartans are your go-to teammates, the ones who show up, adapt, and make things happen. They aim to be their best everyday.

4. Know What Right Looks Like

Experience teaches you what right looks like. It's the wisdom gained from navigating the good, the bad, and the ugly. This insight allows you to identify and correct issues, saving resources and streamlining processes. Knowing what right looks like doesn't happen overnight—it's the result of showing up, learning, and gaining perspective through real-world challenges.

5. Wear Your Body Armor: Perseverance and Resiliency

The more time you spend in the arena, the stronger you become. Resilience and perseverance are your body armor, protecting you as you face challenges and setbacks. Failures aren't the end—they're lessons that make you better. Spartans don't quit; they adjust, adapt, and keep moving forward.

6. Squint with Your Ears

Listening is an underrated but critical skill. Great leaders listen more than they speak. They focus intently on what's being said, translating information into actionable insights. To truly listen, you must block out distractions and avoid multitasking. The best questions often come from those who have taken the time to understand the conversation fully.

7. Push Down Success

Leadership isn't about taking credit—it's about pushing success down to the team. When things go well, recognize those who contributed. When things fall short, take responsibility. This simple practice builds trust, strengthens morale, and sets the standard for true leadership.

8. Build Relationships

In a fast-paced, decentralized world, relationships are more important than ever. Strong relationships provide support, perspective, and collaboration. To build and sustain them, you must show up—physically, emotionally, and mentally. Neglecting relationships leads to disconnection, but investing in them fosters happiness and a sense of belonging.

The Road Ahead

Life's roadmap isn't always clear, but the principles of showing up will guide you. Focus on being your best today while keeping an eye on the future. The Big Eight provides a framework for growth, resilience, and meaningful impact. Follow it, and you'll not only achieve your vision—you'll inspire others to do the same.

15 FINAL THOUGHTS

To be a good Soldier, a successful business leader, a proud parent, talented athlete or reliable friend you Show-up. You prepare, rehearse, and you're ready to engage and be a productive participant in the arena. Here in the arena is where you make a difference. The Arena is your home. Do not associate with those "cold and timid souls who neither know victory nor defeat" (Roosevelt, 1910). Being in cheap seats is easy because it is a position where you just point fingers or regurgitate what you hear from others in the cheap seats.

Time flies by and the obstacle course called Life gets more complex and reveals more options both good and not so good. You have choices and, in some cases, events, outcomes, and decisions take place without your vote.

> BUT BEING PREPARED, KNOWING WHAT RIGHT LOOKS LIKE, AND HAVING YOUR BODY ARMOR (PERSEVERANCE AND PERPETUITY) IS WHAT GETS YOU THROUGH THE MOST CHALLENGING OBSTACLES AND SHINES A LIGHT ON PROGRESS AND OVERALL HAPPINESS.

And like everything there is monetary consideration. However, it is good to prioritize and think through your "return on investment." The best return on investment is when you prioritize monetary expenditures in creating memories and not collecting stuff. Be present and be engaged and you create memories, build trust, and set a positive example for others to follow.

> WHEN YOUR TIME ON THIS PLANET IS OVER, PEOPLE WILL NOT REMEMBER YOU FOR THE HOME YOU LIVED IN, OR THE CAR YOU DROVE, YOUR BANK ACCOUNT, AND THE CLOTHES YOU WORE. THEY WILL REMEMBER YOUR IMPACT ON OTHERS, YOUR PERSEVERANCE AND RESILIENCE, AND YOUR PERSONAL CULTURE OF BEING PREPARED AND ENGAGED. THEY WILL REMEMBER THAT WHEN IT MATTERED MOST, YOU SHOWED UP.

That is your legacy. Don't accept anything less…… Show Up!

ABOUT THE AUTHOR

Charles (Chuck) Anderson is a retired Major General with 32 years of distinguished service in the United States Army, followed by 14 years of leadership in the Federal Services Industry. Over the course of both careers, he has led thousands of soldiers and employees, overseeing complex operations worldwide.

He has lead multi-billion-dollar operations while shaping the next generation of leaders through his unwavering commitment to discipline, resiliency, perseverance, and showing up—the cornerstone of his personal and professional success.

Raised in Ashland, Kentucky, he learned early on the value of hard work, teamwork, and resilience, principles that carried him through West Point, military deployments, and industry. Throughout his military career, he developed as a leader being tactically and technically competent through a combination of education, experience and exposure.

After retiring from active duty, Chuck transitioned seamlessly into the private sector, applying his leadership philosophy to corporate operations, business strategy, and workforce development. He enjoys coaching individuals and organizations on how to achieve success and be resilient during complex and difficult times.

In *Step into the Area—Show Up and Lead*, he delivers no-nonsense, battle-tested wisdom on why success—whether in the military, business, or personal life—comes down to one simple but powerful rule: Show Up. When you Show Up you are prepared both mentally and physically. His book is a call to arms for those who refuse to sit on the sidelines, encouraging others to step into the arena, be at the point of the spear, and lead with unwavering determination.

When he's not inspiring teams and organizations to be resilient he enjoys being with family, friends, and of course, lifting weights and running. Let there be no doubt, Chuck invests time and energy in creating memories and less on "stuff." Show-Up.

www.ingramcontent.com/pod-product-compliance
Lightning Source LLC
Chambersburg PA
CBHW061355010526
44107CB00012B/939